HOW TO WALK IN THE SPIRIT

By BILL BRIGHT

NOTES FOR TEACHERS

A Transferable Concept. Here at your fingertips is a tool that can be used to make disciples of each one in your group. A disciple? Yes. Someone who knows the principles Christ taught in His earthly ministry and has "transferred" or incorporated them into his or her own life. Thus, he has not only grown in the Lord himself, but he is also capable of transferring that concept (or principle) to another and helping him to also grow.

Growth is exciting. It's stimulating. Thought questions and Bible study questions are provided with each section in this booklet so that you have a place to start discussion and stimulate personal growth. This "how to" essential of the Christian life presents tremendous opportunities for teacher and students alike to revitalize their witness, reconsider their priorities and change their world.

Each section should take about 40-50 minutes of teaching time. But this is a general guideline. You can also tailor each lesson to the needs of the group. Students may want to incorporate their own thought questions and delve even deeper into Bible study.

Christians at all stages of maturity in the faith struggle at times. A clearer focus on what's really involved in the Christian walk encourages those who are growing weary in well-doing (often an indication of trying to live the Christian life by self-effort) and excites those who haven't really started walking wholeheartedly with the Lord. This booklet reaches those at all levels of Christian maturity and in every walk of life.

Renewing one's purpose or kindling the fires of faith—this booklet can do either or both.

WHAT IS A TRANSFERABLE CONCEPT?

When our Lord commanded the 11 men to whom He had most shared His earthly ministry to go into all the world and make disciples of all nations, He told them to teach these new disciples all that He had taught them (Matthew 28:18-20).

Later the apostle Paul gave the same instructions to Timothy: "...and the things which you have heard from me...these entrust to faithful men, who will be able to teach others also" (II Timothy 2:2).

In the process of counseling and interacting with tens of thousands of students, laymen and pastors year after year for almost 30 years, our staff have discovered that many church members, including people from churches which honor our Lord and faithfully teach His Word, are not sure of their salvation, that the average Christian is living a defeated and frustrated life and that the average Christian does not know how to share his faith effectively with others.

In our endeavor to help meet these three basic needs and to build Christian disciples, Campus Crusade for Christ, Inc. has developed a series of "how to's"—or "transferable concepts"—in which we discuss many of the basic truths that Jesus and His disciples taught.

A "transferable concept" may be defined as an idea or a truth which can be transferred or communicated from one person to another and then to another, spiritual generation after generation, without distorting or diluting its original meaning.

As these basic truths—"transferable concepts"—of the Christian life are made available through the printed word, films, tapes and cassettes in every major language of the world, they could well be used of God to help transform the lives of tens of millions all over the world.

We encourage you to master each of these concepts until you are personally prepared to communicate them to others "who will be able to teach others also." In so doing, many millions of men and women can be reached and discipled for Christ. They can then · make a significant contribution toward the fulfillment of the Great Commission in our generation.

Contents

Here's Life Publishers
P.O. Box 1576
San Bernardino, CA 92402

Section 1

INTRODUCTION

"Since I have learned how to walk in the Spirit, the Christian life has become a great adventure for me," said a medical doctor after completing his third lay institute for evangelism. "Now, I want everyone to experience this same adventure with Christ."

Would you like to know how to experience a full, abundant, purposeful and fruitful life for Christ? You can! If you have been living in spiritual defeat—impotent and fruitless, wondering if there is any validity to the Christian life—there is hope for you! What greater promise could Christ have possibly offered to the Christian than the assurance that he can walk daily in the power of the Spirit of Jesus Christ and experience an abundant and fruitful life of purpose and adventure.

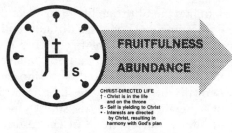

FRUITFULNESS
ABUNDANCE

CHRIST-DIRECTED LIFE
† - Christ is in the life
   and on the throne
S - Self is yielding to Christ
• - Interests are directed
   by Christ, resulting in
   harmony with God's plan

Such ability has been promised by no less an authority than Christ Himself, to all who receive Him as Lord and Savior. Here is His promise: "Truly, truly, I say to you, he who believes in Me, the works that I do shall he do also; and greater works than those shall he do because I go to the Father. And whatever you ask in My name, that will I do, that the Father may be glorified in the Son. If you ask anything in My name, I will do it" (John 14:12-14).

Certain basic spiritual truths, when fully understood and experienced by faith, guarantee revolutionary spiritual benefits. These proven principles can help you to be more consistent in your walk in the Spirit and more effective in your witness for our Savior.

A Supernatural Life

The Christian life, properly understood, is not complex nor difficult. As a matter of fact, the Christian life is very simple. It is so simple that we stumble over the very simplicity of it and yet it is so difficult that no one can live it! This paradox occurs because the Christian life is a supernatural life. The only one who can live it is the Lord Jesus Christ.

If I try to live the Christian life in my own fleshly effort, it does become complex, difficult and even impossible to live. But if I invite the Lord Jesus to direct my life; if I know the reality of having been crucified with Christ and raised with Him by faith as a way of life; if I walk in the light as God is in the light—then the Lord Jesus simply lives His abundant life within me in all of His resurrection power.

This fact was dramatically demonstrated in the lives of the early Christians. When the enemies of the Lord saw the way He was fulfilling His promise in the lives of Peter and John and observed their boldness and the remarkable quality of their lives, they were amazed at these obviously uneducated non-professionals and realized what being with Jesus had done for them (Acts 4:13).

I do not wish to suggest that the Christian who walks in the fullness of the Spirit will have no problems. Problems of poor health, loss of loved ones, financial needs and other such experiences are common to all people. However, most of our problems are self-imposed because of our own carnal, selfish actions. The spiritual man is spared from most of these problems. But when the problems do come, the spiritual man can face them with a calm, confident attitude because he is aware of God's resources which are available to him to deal with such problems.

This is not simply a matter of positive thinking, for we are instructed to cast our cares upon the Lord Jesus because He cares for us (I Peter 5:7). The spiritual man knows the trustworthiness of God from experience. The Lord becomes the problem-solver, and the trials and burdens of this world are no longer too great for us when He is carrying the load.

This was at the heart of the apostle Paul's moment-by-moment experience: "I have been crucified with Christ; and I myself no longer live, but Christ lives in me. And the real life I now have within this body is a result of my trusting in the Son of God, who loved me and gave Himself for me" (Galatians 2:20, Living Bible).

Simple And Understandable

The kind of theology which is so profound that it cannot be understood is not only the product of fuzzy thinking, but it is also a direct contradiction of Scripture. Further, certain teaching to which some refer as the "deeper truths" of the Word often lead to a fascination with these "truths" but do not produce holy lives, fruitful witness or a greater love for Christ and commitment to His cause.

The teaching of the Lord was simple and understandable even though some of the truths which He taught were obscure to men whose eyes were spiritually blind. He spoke of the lilies of the field, the sower and his seed, fishing for men, new wineskins, the vine and the branches—simple lessons that were easily understood by His listeners. Jesus communicated with the people; the "multitudes heard Him gladly," they understood Him, and they followed Him.

In a spiritually illiterate world, we must follow the simplicity of our Savior's message and method if we are to communicate His good news to the multitudes. Since God so loved the people of the world, most of whom have little or no knowledge of spiritual truth, and since He gave His only begotten Son to die for our sins that we may have eternal life, it does not seem reasonable to me that one must be a theologian or even a deep student of the Bible (though this is to be desired) before he can experience and share the abundant life of joy and victory that is our heritage in Christ.

Spiritual Breathing

One of the most important truths of Scripture, the understanding and application of which has enriched my life as has no other truth, is a concept which I like to call "spiritual breathing." This concept has been shared with hundreds of thousands—with revolutionary results—through our literature and various training conferences and seminars.

As you walk in the Spirit by faith, practicing spiritual breathing, you need never again live in spiritual defeat for more than a few minutes at a time. Spiritual breathing, like physical breathing, is a process of exhaling the impure and inhaling the pure, an exercise in faith that enables you to experience God's love and forgiveness as a way of life.

The moment you invited Christ into your life as Savior and Lord, you experienced a spiritual birth. You became a child of God and you were filled with the Holy Spirit. God forgave your sins—past, present and future—making you righteous, holy and acceptable in His sight because of Christ's sacrifice for you on the cross. You were given the power to live a holy life and to be a fruitful witness for God.

Roller Coaster Life

But the average Christian does not understand this concept of spiritual breathing as an exercise of faith and as a result, lives on a spiritual roller coaster. He goes from one emotional experience to another, living most of his life as a carnal Christian, controlling his own life—frustrated and fruitless.

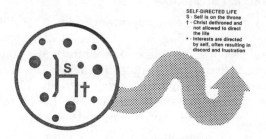

SELF-DIRECTED LIFE
S · Self is on the throne
† · Christ dethroned and not allowed to direct the life
• · Interests are directed by self, often resulting in discord and frustration

If this is your experience, spiritual breathing will enable you to get off this emotional roller coaster and to enjoy the Christian life that the Lord Jesus promised to you when He said, "I came that they might have life and might have it abundantly" (John 10:10, Living Bible). As an exercise in faith, it will enable you to continue to experience God's love, forgiveness and the power and control of the Holy Spirit as a way of life.

Exhale—Confess

If you retake the throne, the control center, of your life through sin—a deliberate act of disobedience—breathe spiritually. First, *exhale by confession*. God's Word promises in I John 1:9, "If we confess our sins, He is faithful and just to forgive us our sins, and to cleanse us from all unrighteousness." Confession (*homologeo* in the Greek) suggests agreement with God concerning our sins. Such agreement involves at least three considerations.

First, you must acknowledge that your sin or sins—which should be named to God specifically— are wrong and are therefore grievous to God. Second, you acknowledge that God has already forgiven you through Christ's death on the cross for your sins. Third, you repent, which means that you change your attitude toward your sin. The power of the Holy Spirit will enable you to change your conduct. Instead of doing what your old sinful nature—your fleshly self—wants to do, you can do what God wants you to do.

Inhale—Appropriate By Faith

Next, *inhale, by appropriating the fullness of God's Spirit by faith.* Trust Him now to control and empower you, according to His command to "be filled with the Spirit" (Ephesians 5:18), which actually means to be *constantly* and *continually* controlled and empowered with the Holy Spirit. According to His promise, he hears us and grants our request because we pray according to His will (I John 5:14, 15). Continue to claim His love, forgiveness and power by faith and continue to have fellowship with Him moment by moment.

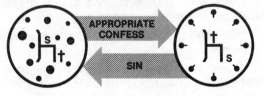

You can get off your spiritual roller coaster, cease to be a carnal Christian and become a Spirit-filled Christian by practicing spiritual breathing. If you are breathing spiritually—exhaling, confessing your sin, and inhaling, appropriating the fullness of the Holy Spirit by faith—you are a Spirit-filled Christian.

Attitude Of Unbelief

What will cause you to become a carnal Christian and fall back into this roller coaster way of life? You become a carnal Christian again when you develop an attitude of unbelief—when you cease to believe the promises of I John 1:9 and I Corinthians 10:13: "No temptation has overtaken you but such as is common to man; and God is faithful, who will not allow you to be tempted beyond what you are able; but with the temptation will provide the way of escape also, that you may be able to endure it."

Paul says in Romans 14:23, "Whatever is not of faith is sin." If you cease to practice spiritual breathing, you will become carnal. You do not become carnal simply by committing one sin or a dozen or a hundred sins provided that you sincerely continue to breathe spiritually. You will become carnal only when you develop an attitude of unbelief and refuse to breathe spiritually.

A man who participated in one of our training conferences a few years ago shared with me his experience when he first realized the practical benefits of spiritual breathing. He had agreed to teach a Sunday school class of young students, and was filled with apprehension because he was not used to teaching students of that age. He planned to arrive at church early in order to make proper preparation for the arrival of his students.

He had asked his family to be ready to leave the house early on that Sunday morning. The family was late getting ready and as he sat in the car in the hot sun, fuming and fussing, waiting for them, he became more and more tense and irritated.

When his family finally got into the car, he exploded with anger, but before he had finished speaking, the Holy Spirit reminded him that his attitude and action did not honor the Lord. Furthermore, he knew that he would be sharing with the children in Sunday school about God's love and forgiveness and patience. By this time he was well aware that he was in no mood for God to use Him.

Changed Attitude

Suddenly he remembered what he had learned about "spiritual breathing." He exhaled by confessing his anger to the Lord, and thanked God that he was already forgiven on the basis of Christ's death for him. Then he apologized to his children, and inhaled by acknowledging afresh the control of the Holy Spirit. He then went on his way rejoicing.

Because he had exhaled—confessed his sin—and inhaled—appropriated the power and acknowledged the control of the Holy Spirit, by faith—his attitude was changed. God was able to use this man to introduce to Christ several young people in his Sunday school class that morning.

Thousands of Christians around the world have shared similar experiences of how this concept of spiritual breathing has brought unusual blessing to their lives and, through them, to the lives of others.

As you exhale and inhale the moment you know that you have sinned, you will recognize greater freedom and power in your life. Simply keep short accounts with God. Do not allow your sins to accumulate.

The Real Evidence

This is not to suggest that we have to sin, but in the words of the apostle John, "My little children, I am telling you this so that you will stay away from sin. But if you sin, there is Someone to plead for you before the Father. His name is Jesus Christ, the one who is all that is good and who pleases God completely.

"He is the one who took God's wrath against our sins upon Himself, and brought us into fellowship with God; and He is the forgiveness for our sins, and not only ours but all the world's. And how can we be sure that we belong to Him? By looking within ourselves: are we really trying to do what He wants us to do?

"Someone may say, 'I am a Christian: I am on my way to heaven; I belong to Christ; but if he doesn't do what Christ tells him to, he is a liar. But those who do what Christ tells them to will learn to love God more and more. That is the way to know whether or not you are a Christian. Anyone who says he is a Christian should live as Christ did" (I John 2:1-6, Living Bible).

Critical And Progressive

You will discover that your relationship with the Holy Spirit is both critical and progressive: critical, in that you discover how to appropriate His power by faith; progressive in that you learn how to grow and mature in the Spirit-controlled walk in faith.

A Christian who has walked in the Spirit by faith for many years will generally demonstrate more of the fruit of the Spirit in his life (Galatians 5:22, 23) and be more fruitful in his witness for Christ than one who has just discovered how to walk in the Spirit. You will become aware of such an area of your life—an attitude or an action—that is displeasing to the Lord. Simply breathe spiritually.

Walking in the Spirit through the practice of spiritual breathing is a simple concept. However, there are four important factors which will contribute greatly to an understanding of this great adventure and insure a successful walk in the Spirit. First, be sure that you are filled with the Holy Spirit. Second, be prepared for spiritual conflict. Third, know your rights as a child of God. And fourth, live by faith. Let us look more closely at each of these factors.

BE SURE: BE PREPARED

First, in order to walk in the Spirit, we must be filled with the Spirit. In Ephesians 5:18, we are admonished, "Be not drunk with wine, wherein is excess; but be filled with the Spirit." To be filled with the Holy Spirit is to be controlled and empowered by the Holy Spirit. We cannot have two masters (Matthew 6:24). There is a throne, a control center, in every life—either self or Christ is on that throne. This concept of Christ being on the throne is so simple that even a child can understand it.

My wife and I began to teach our sons this great truth when they were very young. One evening when we were saying our prayers together, I asked our then eight-year-old son, Zac, "Who is on the throne of your life?" He said, "Jesus." I asked our then five-year-old son, Brad, who was on the throne of his life. He answered "Jesus."

The next morning, their mother had prepared for breakfast a special dish called "egg in a bonnet." It was a delicious, thick piece of french toast with a hole in the middle, and in that hole was a poached egg. As I was enjoying it, I looked over at our young son. He was not eating the egg nor the toast.

I said, "Brad, eat your breakfast." He replied, "I don't want it." "Of course you do," I said. "You'll enjoy it. Look at me; I am enjoying mine." "Well," he said, "I don't like it and I'm not going to eat it." Being a bit dramatic, he began to release a few tears. I had to make up my mind what I was going to do. I could either say to him, "Now young man, you eat that breakfast or else I will spank you;" or reply, "Forget it. I'll eat it myself."

Who's On The Throne?

However, I thought of a better idea. I asked, "Brad, who is on the throne of your life this morning?" At that, the tears really began to pour. He understood the point I was making. He had learned the concept that Christ must be on the throne; but Christ was not on the throne of his life at that moment. When he regained his composure, he replied, in answer to my question, "The devil and me." I asked him, "Whom do you want on the throne?" He answered, "Jesus."

So I said, "Let's pray," and he prayed, "Dear Jesus, forgive me for being disobedient and help me to like this egg." God heard that prayer, and Brad enjoyed his breakfast. As a matter of fact, he ate it all. You see, he had said that he did not like it before he had even tasted it.

That evening as we were saying our prayers, I asked Zac who had been on the throne of his life that day, and he said "Jesus." Then I asked Brad the same question, and he replied, "Jesus. Oh," he added, "except at breakfast this morning."

It is such a simple truth; in its distilled essence, that is what the Christian life is all about—just keeping Christ on the throne. We do this when we understand how to walk in the control and power of the Holy Spirit, for the Holy Spirit came for the express purpose of glorifying Christ by enabling the believer to live a holy life and to be a productive witness for the Savior.

Command And Promise

As I said previously, to be sure we are filled with the Holy Spirit (I Corinthians 3:16), we need to remember two important words: *command*—be ye being filled with—constantly and continually controlled and empowered by—the Holy Spirit; and *promise*—if we ask anything according to God's will, he hears us; and if He hears us, He answers us.

On the authority of God's command we know that we are praying according to His will when we ask Him to fill us—to control and empower us. Therefore, we can expect Him to fill and empower us on the basis of His command and promise, *provided* that we genuinely desire to be filled and trust Him to fill us. Technically, you are filled as an act of faith—not by asking to be filled—in the same way that you became a Christian by faith

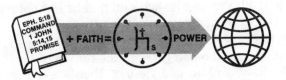

(according to Ephesians 2:8,9) and not merely because you asked Christ to come into your life.

Remember that the Holy Spirit already dwells within you if you are a believer. You do not have to ask Him to come into your life; He is already indwelling you. Your body is a temple of God from the moment you became a Christian. So you simply say to Him, "I surrender my life to You, and by faith I appropriate Your fullness."

The Spirit Reveals Sin

Then continue to breathe spiritually, exhaling whenever the Holy Spirit reveals sin that you need to confess and inhaling as you go on walking in the fullness and control of the Spirit by faith. Some Christians breathe spiritually faster and more often than others.

Exhale only when the Holy Spirit reveals something that needs to be confessed. For some that could be several times each day, while for others it will only be a few times a year.

Avoid being introspective. Do not probe within yourself, looking for sin to confess. Confess only what the Holy Spirit impresses you to confess. Believe God and His Word. Do not seek an emotional experience. If you genuinely hunger and thirst after God and His righteousness; if you have confessed your sin, surrendered the control of your life to Christ and asked God to fill you, believe that you are filled by faith on the basis of His promise. God will prove Himself faithful to His promise.

Fact, Faith, Feeling

Do not depend upon feelings. The promise of God's Word, not our feelings, is our authority. The Christian is to live by faith, trusting in the trustworthiness of God Himself and His Word. This can be illustrated by a train. Let us call the engine *fact*—the fact of God's promises found in His Word. The coal car we will call *faith*—our trust in God and His Word. The caboose we will call *feelings*.

You place coal in the engine and the train runs. However, it would be futile to attempt to pull the train by the caboose. In the same way we, as Christians should not depend upon feelings or emotions, but in order to live a Spirit-filled life should simply place our faith in the trustworthiness of God and the promises of His Word. Feelings are like the caboose—they will eventually come along in the life of faith, but we should never depend on feelings or look for them. The very act of looking for an emotional experience is a denial of the concept of faith, and whatever is not of faith is sin.

FACT   FAITH   FEELING

You can know right now that you are filled with the Spirit by trusting in God, His command and promise, and you can go through life with that assurance. In order to walk in the Spirit, then, we must first be filled and then we must continue to breathe spiritually.

Be Prepared For Spiritual Conflict

Second, we must be prepared for spiritual conflict if we expect to walk in the control—the fullness and power—of the Holy Spirit. As we have already considered, the Christian life is a supernatural life, and the only one who can live it is Christ. We must be prepared for spiritual conflict, but we should remember that for the Christian the battle is not ours but the Lord's. He promises to fight for us (Exodus 14:14).

The Bible explains that there are three forces—the world, the flesh and the devil—which are constantly waging battle against the believer.

The World

The Bible warns us in I John 2:15-17, "Stop loving this evil world and all that it offers you, for when you love these things you show that you do not really love God; for all these worldly things, these evil desires—the craze for sex, the ambition to buy everything that appeals to you, and the pride that comes from wealth and importance— these are not from God. They are from this evil world itself. And this world is fading away, and these evil, forbidden things are going with it, but whoever keeps doing the will of God will live forever" (Living Bible).

I do not know anyone who loves this world who has ever been used of God in any significant way. There is nothing wrong with money and other material success. However, we are to wear the cloak of materialism loosely. We are to set our affection on Christ and His kingdom, not on the material things of this world. "But take courage; I have overcome the world" (John 16:33).

The Flesh

External forces without and internal forces within us are constantly fighting to win control over us, and we are never free from their pressure. "For the flesh (the old sin nature) sets its desire against the Spirit, and the Spirit against the flesh; for those are in opposition to one another, so that you may not do the things that you please" (Galatians 5:17).

This conflict in our lives will continue so long as we live. There will never be a time when we are free from temptation. All people, no matter how spiritual they are, are tempted and have a tendency toward sin.

There is a difference between temptation and sin. Temptation is the initial impression to do something contrary to God's will. Such impressions come to all men and women, even as they did to the Lord, and are not sin in themselves. Temptation becomes sin when we meditate on the impression and develop a desire which becomes lust and is often followed by the actual act of disobedience.

Yet, this major conflict is largely resolved, when we, by an act of the will, surrender ourselves to the control of the Holy Spirit and face these temptations in His power. "Walk by the Spirit and you will not carry out the desire of the flesh" (Galatians 5:16). For practical daily living we simply recognize our weakness whenever we are tempted and ask the Lord to take care of the problem for us.

The Devil

We are told in I Peter 5:7,8 to let God have all of our worries and cares, for He is always thinking about us and watching everything that concerns us. We are to be careful—watching out for attacks from Satan, our great enemy, who prowls around like a hungry roaring lion, looking for some victim to tear apart. Satan is a real foe—let there be no mistake about it—and we need to be alert to his cunning and subtle ways, as well as his obvious attempts to defeat and destroy us.

A young minister shared with me one day, "I am afraid of Satan." I said, "You should be afraid of Satan, if you insist on controlling your own life. But if you are willing to let Christ control your life, you have nothing to fear because the Bible says 'Greater is He who is in you than he who is in the world.' " (I John 4:4, Living Bible).

"Satan was defeated 2,000 years ago when Christ in fulfillment of prophecy died on the cross for our sins. Though Satan has great power to influence man, he has only that power which God has granted to him. That is why, in the face of great persecution, the disciples could pray to God in His sovereignty and power, 'They won't stop at anything that You in Your wise power will let them do'" (Acts 4:28, Living Bible).

Stay Out Of The Cage

My minister friend happened to live in a city with one of the largest zoos in the world. I said, "What do you do with lions in your city?" He replied, "We put them in a cage." I said, "Satan is in a cage. Visit the cage in the zoo and watch a lion pacing impatiently back and forth. He cannot hurt you. Even if you go up close to the cage, he still cannot hurt you if you are careful. But stay out of that cage, or you will be in trouble. Get in the cage, and the lion will make mincemeat of you. But you have nothing to fear as long as you stay out of that cage.

"Similarly, you have nothing to fear from Satan as long as you depend upon Christ and not on your own strength. Remember, Satan has no power except that which God in His wisdom allows him to have."

The apostle Paul warns us, "Put on all of God's armor so that you will be able to stand safe against the strategies and tricks of Satan. For we are not fighting people made of flesh and blood, but against persons without bodies—the evil rulers of the unseen world, those mighty satanic beings and great evil princes of darkness who rule this world; and against huge numbers of wicked spirits in the spirit world" (Ephesians 6:11,12, Living Bible).

Satan and the forces of darkness are real foes. We must be alert to the way Satan works, but we need not be afraid. We need have no fear of him—if we are willing to trust the Lord—even though he is an expert at inducing Christians to disobey God. But if we continue to be carnal Christians, we had better be ready for some real problems in our individual lives and in our churches.

Section 1

1. What does John 14:12-14 mean to you?

   _____

   _____

   _____

2. What does being crucified with Christ mean?
   (See Galatians 2:20.)

   _____

   _____

   _____

3. How do the accounts of the following people
   demonstrate their walk in the Spirit?

   Paul—Acts 18:4-11 (cf. Philippians 4): _____

   _____

   Peter—Acts 3:1-26 (cf. Acts 4:13): _____

   _____

   Stephen—Acts 6:8-15 (cf. 7:51-60): _____

   _____

4. a) What does it mean to you to cast your cares
   upon the Lord (I Peter 5:7)?

   _____

   _____

   b) How can you do this?

   _____

   _____

5. What does the example of the vine and branches
   in John 15:1-8 mean to you in your Christian
   life?

   _____

   _____

   _____

6. How would you describe the effects of spiritual
   fitness as expressed in "spiritual breathing?"

   Romans 14:23 _____

   _____

   I John 1:9 _____

   _____

I Corinthians 10:13 _____

_____

Ephesians 5:18 _____

_____

I John 5:14,15 _____

_____

7. What promise does God make to you in I John 2:1-6?

_____

_____

8. a) In what areas of your life is "self" on the throne?

_____

  b) In what areas of you life is Jesus on the throne?

_____

  c) What are you going to do about those areas in which "self" is still in control?

_____

_____

9. a) What concrete examples from your life can you give that show the presence of fact, faith and feelings?

_____

_____

_____

b) What were the results of putting faith in your feelings rather than in the fact of God and His Word?

_____

_____

10. What armor used to defend yourself against the world, flesh and devil does Ephesians 6:11-18 describe?

_____

_____

Section 2
KNOW YOUR RIGHTS

If we are going to walk in the Spirit, we need to know our rights as children of God. We need to know our spiritual heritage. We need to know how to draw upon the inexhaustible resources of God's love, power, forgiveness and abundant grace.

One of the most important things we can do to learn who God is, who man is and what our rights are is to spend much time—even at a sacrifice of other needs and demands on our schedules—in reading, studying, memorizing and meditating on the Word of God, and in prayer and witnessing.

Balanced Life

It is impossible to walk vigorously and contagiously in the Spirit without spending time, unhurried time, in fellowship with the Lord in His Word—in prayer and in personal study. We must listen sensitively to Him for His directions for our daily activities as a basis for our daily witness for Christ.

On the other hand, I would hasten to emphasize that, without the regular sharing of your faith in Christ with others, Bible study and prayer can often lead to a spiritually frustrating and impotent life. After many years of working with thousands of Christians, I am convinced that one cannot enjoy the full and abundant life which is our heritage in Christ apart from the proper balance between Bible study, prayer and sharing Christ with others out of the overflow of an obedient, Spirit-filled life. We need to be able not only to experience this great adventure with Christ for ourselves, but also to share this good news with others.

A word of caution is in order at this point. We become spiritual, experience power from God and become fruitful in our witness as a result of faith and faith alone. The Bible clearly teaches that "just shall live by faith." Works are the result of faith.

Result Of Faith

Many Christians are confused on this point. They think of works (Bible study, prayer and other spiritual disciplines) as the means to—rather than the results of—the life of faith. They spend much time in Bible study and prayer. They may even attempt to witness for Christ and to obey the various commands of God, thinking that by these means they will achieve the abundant Christian life. But they remain defeated, frustrated, impotent and fruitless. Feeling that their problem is that they must not be doing enough, they then spend even more time in prayer and Bible study—all to no avail and leading to even greater frustration and defeat.

Bible study, prayer, witnessing and obedience are the result of the life of faith, not the means to it. As you are filled with the Holy Spirit, the Bible comes alive, prayer becomes vital, your witness becomes effective and obedience becomes a joy. As a result of your obedience in these various areas, your faith grows and you become more mature in your spiritual life. James 2:22 says, concerning the life of Abraham, "You see, he was trusting God so much that He was willing to do whatever God told him to do; his faith was made complete by what he did, by his actions, his good deeds" (Living Bible).

Yes, Bible study, prayer and obedience are important, vitally important, but they should be regarded as the result—the overflow—of the life of faith, not as the means to faith.

Strength In Christ

Paul says, "I want to remind you that your strength must come from the Lord's mighty power within you" (Ephesians 6:10, Living Bible). Jesus Christ, in all of His mighty resurrection power, lives in all of us who have become children of God through faith in Christ (Romans 8; Ephesians 1:19-25; Colossians 1:27-2:10). I do not have any strength in myself.

As a young man in college and later in business, I used to be very self-efficient—proud of what I could do on my own. I believed that a man could do just about anything he wanted to do on his own if he was willing to pay the price of hard work and sacrifice, and I experienced some degree of success. Then, when I became a Christian, I was introduced to a whole new philosophy of life—a life of trusting replaced my life of trying.

Now I realize how totally incapable I am of living the Christian life—how weak I am in my own strength and yet how strong I am in Christ. As Paul said, "I can do all things through him (Christ) who strengthens me" (Philippians 4:13). "God has not given us a spirit of fear; but of power and of love, and of a sound mind" (II Timothy 1:7, King James).

"Greater is He who is in you than he who is in the world" (I John 4:4, Living Bible).

In John 15:4,5, the Lord stresses the importance

of drawing our strength from Him: "Take care to live in Me, and let me live in you. For a branch cannot produce fruit when severed from the vine. Nor can you be fruitful apart from Me. Yes, I am the vine; you are the branches. Whoever lives in Me and I in him shall produce a large crop of fruit. For apart from Me, you can't do a thing" (Living Bible).

In our own strength we are helpless, impotent, fruitless; we are like branches cut off from the vine if we try to live our own lives, even as Christians. But if we abide in Christ, and He abides in us, it is His life-giving power that is expressed through us and enables us to live and witness for him.

Fishing For Men

Jesus explained the importance of a fruitful witness in John 15:8: "By this is My Father glorified, that you bear much fruit, and so prove to be My disciples." In Matthew 4:19 He says, "Follow Me, and I will make you fishers of men." It is our responsibility to follow Him. It is His responsibility to make us fishers of men. What a relief to know that the responsibility of bearing fruit is the Lord's.

All that God expects of us is our availability, our trust and our obedience. We are to live holy lives and tell others about Christ at every opportunity — but their response is dependent upon the working of the Holy Spirit in their lives. Success in witnessing is simply sharing Christ in the power of the Holy Spirit and leaving the results to God.

Work Of The Spirit

I have never led anyone to Christ and I never shall, though I have had the privilege of praying with thousands who have received Christ as a result of my witness. This is the work of the Holy Spirit. Therefore I cannot boast over much fruit or be discouraged over little fruit. The responsibility for fruit belongs to the Holy Spirit, who works in and through me, producing fruit and changing the lives of individuals.

Christ's power is available to all who trust Him. Paul writes, "I pray that you will begin to understand how incredibly great His power is to help those who believe Him. It is that same mighty power that raised Christ from the dead and seated Him in the place of honor at God's right hand in heaven, far, far above any other king or ruler or dictator or leader.

"Yes, His honor is far more glorious than that of anyone else either in this world or in the world to

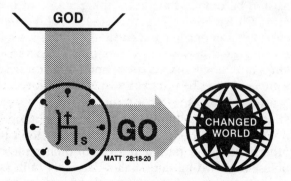

come. And God has put all things under His feet and made Him the supreme Head of the church—which is His Body, filled with Himself, the Author and Giver of everything everywhere" (Ephesians 1:19-23, Living Bible).

I Am With You Always

The Lord Jesus commissioned the disciples to go into all the world and preach the gospel, with the promise that He would always be with them. He said, "I have been given all authority in heaven and earth. Therefore go and make disciples in all the nations . . . and then teach these new disciples to obey all the commands I have given you" (Matthew 28:18-20, Living Bible).

He did not say to them, "Go into all the world, and good luck." He said, "And be sure of this—that I am with you always, even to the end of the world" (Matthew 28:18-20). "I will never, never fail you nor forsake you" (Hebrews 13:5, Living Bible).

Our living Savior, the one whom we serve, is the omnipotent God! He is the one who the Bible tells us "is the exact likeness of the unseen God. He existed before God made anything at all, and, in fact, Christ Himself is the creator who made everything in heaven and earth, the things we can see and the things we can't; the spirit world and its kings and kingdoms, its rulers and authorities: all were made by Christ for His own use and glory . . .

"For God wanted all of Himself to be in His Son . . . In Him lie hidden all the mighty untapped treasures of wisdom and knowledge . . . Don't let others spoil your faith and joy with their philosophies, their wrong and shallow answers built on men's thoughts and ideas, instead of on what Christ has said.

"For in Christ there is all of God in a human body; so you have everything when you have Christ, and you are filled with God through your union with Christ. He is the highest ruler with authority

over every other power" (Colossians 1:15,16,19;
2:3,8-10, Living Bible).

Every Need Supplies

If we have Christ, we have everything we need,
for, as Paul writes to the Colossian church, we are
complete in Him. According to your day, so shall
strength be given. Do you need love? Our Lord
Jesus Christ is the incarnation of love. Do you
need joy? He is joy. Do you need peace? Christ is
peace. Do you need patience? Christ is patience.
Do you need wisdom? Christ is wisdom.

Are you in need of material possessions so that
you can better serve Christ? They are available in
Him. He owns the cattle on a thousand hills, and I
would remind you of His promise to supply the
needs of all who trust him. Christianity is Christ,
and you are complete in Him. He is all you need.

Knowing Christ Better

Therefore, every Christian should give priority
to seeking to know Him better. We do this largely
through spending much time with Him in reading
and meditating on His Word, talking to Him in
prayer, obeying His commands and telling others
about Him. We cannot really get to know Him well
if any one of these three elements is missing from
our daily lives.

For example, consider and meditate on this
exciting passage from Romans that explains the
practical benefits every believer can experience
because of Christ's death for us on the cross. Paul
writes:

"Adam caused many to be sinners because he

disobeyed God, and Christ caused many to be acceptable to God because he obeyed. The Ten Commandments were given so that all could see the extent of their failure to obey God's laws. But the more we see our sinfulness, the more we see God's abounding grace forgiving us.

"Before, sin ruled over all men and brought them to death, but now God's kindness rules instead, giving us right standing with God and resulting in eternal life through Jesus Christ our Lord.

Sin's Power Broken

"Well then, shall we keep on sinning so that God can keep on showing us more and more kindness and forgiveness? Of course not! Should we keep on sinning when we don't have to? For sin's power over us was broken when we became Christians and were baptized to become a part of Jesus Christ: through his death the power of your sinful nature was shattered... Your old evil desires were nailed to the cross with Him; that part of you that loves to sin was crushed and fatally wounded, so that your sin-loving body is no longer under sin's control, no longer needs to be a slave to sin.

"So look upon your old sin nature as dead and unresponsive to sin, and instead be alive to God, alert to Him... Do not let any part of your bodies become tools of wickedness to be used for sinning; but give yourselves completely to God—every part of you—for you are back from death and you want to be tools in the hands of God, to be used for his good purposes... Don't you realize that you can choose your own master? You can choose sin (with death) or else obedience (with acquittal). The one

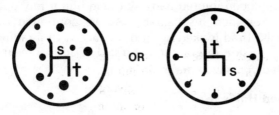

to whom you offer yourself—He will take you and be your master and you will be His slave" (Romans 5:19-21; 6:1-3, 6, 11, 13, 16, Living Bible).

Oh, how wonderful to know that these members of our bodies—our eyes, our ears, our lips, our hands, our feet—can be used for the glory of God.

We Do Not Become Puppets

A student asked, "If I give my life to Christ, will I become a puppet?" No. We never become puppets. We have the right to choose—we are free moral agents. God guides and encourages us, but we must act. He does not force us. But the more we understand the love of God, the faithfulness of God and the power of God, the more we will want to trust Him with every detail of our lives. The secret of the successful Christian life is to keep Christ on the throne of our lives. We shall fail in the Christian life only if we as a deliberate act of our wills choose to be disobedient.

One day my wife, Vonette, and I were wading down a shallow stream in Yosemite Park with our two sons. Because the rocks were slippery I was holding my five-year-old, Bradley, by the hand to keep him from slipping on the rocks. Suddenly Brad did slip and his feet went out from under him. We would have had a serious fall and could have been injured had I not held him firmly until he regained his balance. As we continued our walk, Brad looked up into my face with a radiant expression of gratitude and said "Daddy, I'm sure glad you saved me from falling."

God Holds Us

In the flash of a moment, it was as though God had spoken to me, and I looked up to Him and said, "Father, I am so glad that you have me by the hand. How many times You have kept me from falling!" Oh, this Christian life is wonderful. It is exciting! It is filled with adventure for those who let God control their lives—who walk with Him moment by moment, day by day, allowing Him to "hold their hands."

This personal, intimate walk with Christ, our Savior and our friend, is Christianity—not the struggle, the strain, the labor, the self-disciplining which is usually characteristic of the average, misinformed Christian. If you desire to walk in the Spirit, be sure to know your rights as a child of God, so that you can say with the apostle Paul, "I can do all things through Him (Christ) who strengthens me" (Philippians 4:13).

Section 2

1. What does prayer mean to you?

_____

_____

2. What do these verses say about prayer?

Hebrews 4:15,16 _____

_____

James 5:16 _____

_____

I Samuel 12:23 _____

_____

James 1:5 _____

_____

3. a) How do you achieve the abundant Christian
   life?

   _____

   _____

b) Does "abundant" mean that your life will be free from struggles and hardships? Explain.

_____

_____

4. What do these verses say about witnessing?

Acts 1:8 _____

_____

Matthew 28:18-20 _____

_____

John 15:8 _____

_____

Matthew 4:19 _____

_____

5. How can you break sin's power in your life?

_____

_____

6. What do these verses promise you if you trust God?

Job 12:9,10 _____

Psalm 16:1,11 _____

_____

Psalm 16:1,11 _____

_____

Ecclesiastes 2:24-26 _____

_____

Isaiah 40:10,11 _____

_____

Isaiah 41:10 _____

_____

Section 3
LIVE BY FAITH

If we are to walk in the Spirit, we must live by faith. Oh, how sad to see wonderful, sincere Christians who have been deceived by a wrong emphasis on emotions. I know of nothing else that has caused so much defeat among Christians. We do not live by feelings. We live by faith. According to Hebrews 11:6, "Without faith it is impossible to please Him." In Galatians 3:11, Paul reminds us, "We live by faith."

Valid emotional feelings are simply the byproduct of faith and obedience. There is nothing wrong with feelings. Thank God we have them. Do not be ashamed of feelings, but do not seek them. Never emphasize them. To seek an emotional experience repudiates the command to live by faith and is, in fact, an insult to God. Let emotions find their proper place in your relationship with Christ.

John 14:21 indicates that the most valid way to have an emotional experience is to be obedient to Christ. Jesus said, "He who has my commandments and keeps them, he it is who loves Me, and he who loves Me shall be loved by My Father, and I will love him, and will disclose (make real) Myself to him."

Emotional Counterfeits

One of the greatest acts of obedience is to share Christ with others in the power of the Holy Spirit. Since He came to seek and to save the lost and has commissioned us to witness for Him, nothing could please the Savior more. If you want a valid, vital, exciting awareness of Christ in your experience, begin to share Christ with others as a way of life as you walk in the Spirit.

Avoid man-made emotionalism that is generated by resorting to tricks and manipulations of individuals. Many such emotional experiences are a counterfeit of the genuine experience which can be yours through obedience to Christ, our Savior.

We live according to God's promise, trusting in the integrity of God Himself. Faith must have an object, and the object of our faith is God, made known through His Word. God has proven Himself to be worthy of our trust. There are thousands of promises for us contained in God's Word, and no Christian has ever found any one of them to be untrue. When God says something, you can stake your life on it—you can know that He will not fail you.

Thanksgiving Demonstrates Faith

In Romans 8:28 we read one of God's promises to us: "All things work together for good to those who love God, to those who are the called according to His purpose." Do you believe this promise of God? If so, you logically acknowledge the reasonableness of the command of God in I Thessalonians 5:18: "In everything give thanks; for this is God's will for you in Christ Jesus."

Have you learned to say, "Thank You, Lord," when your heart is broken because of the loss of a loved one? Do you thank God when your body is wracked with pain? When you receive a "Dear John" letter terminating a love relationship? When you have financial reverses? When you fail an exam? When you are unemployed? Do you thank

God when you are discriminated against personally, religiously or racially?

You may say that only a fool would give thanks to God under such circumstances. No, not if "all things work together for good to those who love God, to those who are called according to His purpose." If God has commanded us to give thanks, there is a reason for it. This is one of the most exciting lessons I have ever learned—the lesson of saying "Thank You" when things go wrong.

A Better Plan

Before I made this discovery I used to lose my patience when things went contrary to my wishes. Closed doors would often be forced open, if necessary. If they did not open before me, I tried to break them down. I was often tense inside and impatient with others. Then I discovered what a fool I was. Tragically we injure our brothers with our impatience, our criticism, our thoughtlessness. When Christians act this way, the entire Body of Christ suffers.

But God has given us a better plan. We can relax. We can say "Thank You" when the whole world is crumbling around us, because our God is sovereign and omnipotent. He holds the world in His hands, and we can trust Him. He loves us. And He promises to fight for us.

He has commanded us to cast all of our cares upon Him, for He cares for us (I Peter 5:7). He personally visited Earth and took our sins upon Himself, and He is waiting to bless and use us. But He will not bless and use us if we are worried and unbelieving. He will not bless and use us if we complain and criticize and find fault.

Some time ago, a young woman came to Arrowhead Springs for one of our training institutes. After one of my lectures, she came for counsel. Through her tears she shared how her dearest friend had been killed in an accident. The young woman had been driving the car when he was killed. They were coming home from their engagement party, and an oncoming automobile crossed the center line, forcing her off the road into a telephone pole.

The tragedy was compounded by the guilt she felt because she had been driving the car. Her heart was broken. "What shall I do?" she pleaded.

Have You Thanked God?

Months had passed and she had gone to psychiatrists, psychologists, ministers and many others seeking counsel. She said, "If you can't help me, I fear for my sanity." I asked her if she were a Christian, and she said, "Yes." We read Romans 8:28 and I asked her, "Do you believe that all things work for good?" She said, "Yes, I believe that."

We turned to I Thessalonians 5:18. She read it aloud: "In all things give thanks, for this is the will of God in Christ Jesus concerning you." I said to her, "Have you thanked God for the loss of your loved one?" She was shocked and could hardly believe she heard me correctly. Looking at me in disbelief, she said, "How can I thank God for such a tragic loss?"

"You do not trust God, do you?" I asked. "Yes, I trust God," she insisted. "Then why not show that you do?" I asked. "Will you pray and tell God that you trust Him and give thanks in everything?" As we knelt together, she prayed through her tears, "God I don't understand, but I know I can trust You; and I do say, 'Thank You.'"

Demonstrating Faith

When she said, "Thank You," she was saying to God, "I will trust You." The Bible says that without faith you cannot please God (Hebrews 11:6) and the best way to demonstrate faith is to say, "Thank You." You may think that you hate God because you have lost a loved one, your inheritance, your money, your business or your health. You may ask, "Why did God do this to me?" But God says, "In everything give thanks." Unbelief is sin and displeases God, according to Hebrews 3:17-4:2 and Romans 14:23.

That young lady came to my office early the next morning literally bubbling with joy. She said, "Last night I slept without medication for the first time since the accident. And this morning when I awakened, my heart was filled with praise and thanksgiving to God. I just cannot understand it, but I know that it has something to do with what you taught me about saying 'Thank You' to God." I could share hundreds of similar stories about Christians whose lives have been transformed by learning the simple lesson of saying "Thank You" in all things.

Some years ago there was a desperate need for more than a half million dollars toward the purchase of Arrowhead Springs, the Campus Crusade for Christ International Headquarters. The future of a great worldwide ministry was at stake. Because of a technicality, our financial world had crumbled, and there appeared to be no hope. The whole ministry was in danger of being destroyed and my own reputation would be shattered.

When word came to me from a friend that the money which we had been promised was no longer available, I fell to my knees and said, "Lord, what am I to do?" I opened my Bible to look for help and assurance. And I was reminded that all things work together for good to those who love God, that without faith, it is impossible to please Him, and that the just shall live by faith. I read the command from God to give thanks in everything.

God is Faithful

So I got back down on my knees and thanked God for what had happened. I thanked Him through my tears. I thanked Him that in His wisdom and love, He knew better than I what should be done and that out of this chaos and uncertainty would come a miraculous solution to our problem. There on my knees, while I was giving thanks for the disappointment I was feeling, God began to give me the genuine assurance that a miracle was really going to happen. Within ten days God did provide an almost unbelievable solution to our problem—a miracle. He demonstrated again that, when we trust Him, He is faithful and worthy of our trust.

Trust God More

One of the greatest privileges is to trust God. Learn how to walk by faith. I am still learning and am confident that one day I shall be able to trust God for infinitely greater things than those for which I am now able to trust Him. What a great opportunity is ours to walk with the King of kings every day of our lives, from the time that we awaken in the morning until we go to bed at night.

For many years it has been my practice to begin my day the night before by reading God's Word, meditating upon the attributes and trustworthiness of our wonderful Lord before I go to sleep at night. Then throughout the nightwatches, when my subconscious mind takes over, I am thinking about Christ. When I awaken in the morning, my first thoughts are of Him.

I usually awaken with a psalm of praise on my lips, and with an attitude of thanksgiving: "Oh, Lord, I thank You that I belong to You. I thank You that You live within me, and I thank You that you have forgiven my sins. I thank You that I am a child of God.

"Now, as I begin this day, and as I continue throughout the day, I thank You that You walk around in my body, love with my heart, speak with my lips and think with my mind. I thank You that, You promised to do greater things through me than You did when You were here on the earth. By faith, I acknowledge Your greatness, Your power, Your authority in my life, and I invite You to do anything You wish in and through me."

Then I slip out of bed to my knees, as a formal act of acknowledging His lordship. I try to begin the day right, walking in the fullness of His power. What an adventure awaits those who trust the Lord.

Moment By Moment

In summary, may I remind you that if you desire

to walk moment by moment, day by day, in the fullness and power of God's Spirit, you must:

First, be sure that you are filled with the Spirit, by faith—on the basis of God's command to be filled and by claiming His promise that, if we ask according to His will, He will hear and answer.

Second, be prepared for spiritual conflict. The enemy is a real foe to be reckoned with. The world, the flesh and the devil will assail.

Third, know your rights as a child of God. Our strength must come from the Lord. We must abide in Him.

And finally, live by faith, drawing daily upon His strength, His wisdom, His power and His love, giving thanks in all things.

Why should a Christian desire to walk in the fullness and control of the Holy Spirit moment by moment as a way of life? There are several important reasons: to please and honor the Lord, who delights to have fellowship with His children; to enjoy a fuller, richer, more exciting life with our Savior and with others; and to be more fruitful in our witness for our Savior.

Sharing Christ with others as an expression of gratitude and as an act of obedience to the Lord is the natural result of walking in the fullness of the Holy Spirit.

We are commanded to be witnesses for the Lord; therefore, not to be so involved and committed is to disobey Him and would indicate that the Christian is not walking in the control of the Holy Spirit.

Continue To Breathe Spiritually

As you walk in the Spirit and faithfully apply the revolutionary concept of spiritual breathing, you can become a member of the great army of effective Christian disciples whom God is raising up around the world to work, to plan, to pray and to witness for Christ—to help fulfill the Great Commission of our Lord in this generation.

Section 3

1. What place do feelings have in a life of faith?

   _____

   _____

2. What do these verses say about thanksgiving?

   I Thessalonians 5:18 _____

   _____

   Philippians 4:11 _____

   _____

   Ephesians 5:20 _____

   _____

   Psalm 95:2 _____

   _____

   Philippians 4:6 _____

   _____

3. a) How does Romans 8:28 have *practical* meaning
   in your life?

   _____

   _____

   b) What are some of the consequences of *not*
   applying this verse?

   _____

   _____

4. What does it mean to trust God and walk moment
   by moment with Him?

   _____

   _____

5. What condition and promise did God make to
   you in I John 5:14?

   _____

   _____

6. What does John 14:21 tell you about how to
   have an obedient walk with Christ?

   _____

   _____

STUDY GUIDE

1. Read this booklet and/or listen to the cassette tape of this Concept for six consecutive days. Educational research has shown that it is necessary to read or hear a Concept six to ten times to understand it thoroughly. Think through the questions at the end of each section each time you read the concept. The application of the principles outlined in this Concept will enable you to live a Spirit-controlled life consistently as a way of life.

2. Memorize the following verses and references:

   Galatians 5:22,23: "But the fruit of the Spirit is love, joy, peace, patience, kindness, goodness, faithfulness, gentleness, self-control; against such things there is no law."

   I Thessalonians 5:18: "In everything give thanks; for this is God's will for you in Jesus Christ."

   Your memory work will be easier and more lasting if you review it daily for the entire week rather than try to complete it in just one day.

3. Work the review questions at the end of each section, looking up the Scripture references and filling in the blanks with your answers.

4. Participate in a group discussion using the Bible study. If you are not already a part of a Bible study or some other group that is studying the Transferable Concepts, form your own group by inviting others to join you in your study program. As you discuss the Bible study questions, share what God is teaching you about how to walk moment by moment in the fullness of the Holy Spirit. Share, also, how you plan to apply the principles in this Concept to your life and how you plan to share them with others.

5. Finally, make this Concept, "How to Walk in the Spirit," a way of life through practicing the following:

   a. Begin each day by praying and by reading or studying God's Word, as time allows. Make sure that you are filled with the Holy Spirit as you begin each day. During the day, whenever you find yourself back in control of your life with self on the throne, breathe spiritually: exhale—confess your sin, and inhale—appropriate again the fullness of the Holy Spirit.

   b. Conclude your day by thanking God for enabling you to walk in the Spirit during the day, and by reading God's Word and praying.

   c. Make a point of giving thanks as an expression of your faith for every difficult situation that comes your way during each day, as well as for the blessings.

   d. Use the brief outline in the front of this booklet, the amplified outline in the back, or a tape recording of this Concept as a means of sharing this vital truth with other people. Share it as often as you can throughout the week. Provide a booklet for those with whom you share this Concept so that they, too, can study this material in depth and pass it on to others also.

AMPLIFIED OUTLINE

A. Every person can experience a full, abundant, purposeful and meaningful life (John 14:12-14).

B. The Christian life is not complex or difficult, but there is a paradox to it.

   1. It is so simple that we stumble over its simplicity.

   2. It is so difficult—because it is a supernatural life—that only Christ can live it.

C. The secret of the Christian life is to walk in the Spirit and thus allow the Lord Jesus to live His abundant life within us in all of His resurrection power (Acts 4:13).

D. Even the Christian has problems, but he can freely cast all of these problems on the Lord (I Peter 5:7; Galatians 2:20).

E. The teachings of our Lord are simple and understandable.

F. Spiritual breathing is the key to our appropriating God's spiritual provision for us moment by moment.

   1. When we receive Christ as our personal Savior, we experience a spiritual birth, we become children of God, our sins are forgiven and we are filled with the Spirit.

   2. The average Christian is not drawing on his resources in Christ, but is living on a spiritual roller coaster going from one emotional experience to another, in control of his own life frustrated and defeated.

G. "Spiritual breathing" will enable us to get off this emotional roller coaster and to enjoy the abundant Christian life Jesus promised (John 10:10).

1. Exhale by confessing our sins (agreeing with God concerning them) (I John 1:9).

   a. Acknowledge—agree with God—that our sins are wrong

   b. Acknowledge—agree with God—that Christ has already forgiven us because of Christ's death on the cross for our sins.

   c. Repent, or change our attitude toward our sin, and experience a change in our conduct through the enabling power of the Holy Spirit.

2. Inhale by appropriating the fullness of God's Spirit by faith.

   a. His command, and thus His will, is that we can be filled with the Spirit (Ephesians 5:18).

   b. His promise is that He always grants our requests when we pray according to His will (I John 5:14,15).

H. A spiritual Christian becomes a carnal Christian again when he ceases to believe I Corinthians 10:13 and I John 1:9—when he develops an attitude of unbelief (Romans 14:23b).

I. We should not allow sins to accumulate in our lives (I John 2:1-6).

J. Our relationship with the Holy Spirit is both critical and progressive.

K. A spiritual Christian will demonstrate the fruit of the Spirit in his life (Galatians 5:22,23).

I. BE SURE THAT YOU ARE FILLED WITH THE HOLY SPIRIT.

A. In Ephesians 5:18 we are commanded to be filled with the Spirit which means to be controlled and empowered by the Holy Spirit.

B. Either Christ or self is on the throne, and in control, of our lives, for no man can serve two masters.

C. Remember two important words in order to be sure that you are filled with the Holy Spirit.

  1. *Command*—be filled with the Spirit (Ephesians 5:18).

  2. *Promise*—if we ask anything according to God's will He hears and answers (I John 5:14,15).

D. We are filled with the Spirit by faith, just as we received Christ by faith (Ehpesians 2:8,9) and not just because we ask Him into our lives.

E. If you are a Christian, you are already indwelt by the Holy Spirit (I Corinthians 3:16), so you simply need to ask Him to take control of your life, and then continue to breathe spiritually whenever the Holy Spirit reveals something you need to confess.

F. Do not look for nor depend upon feelings.

II. BE PREPARED FOR SPIRITUAL CONFLICT.

  A. Though we must be prepared for spiritual conflict, we must also remember that the battle is not ours, but the Lord's (Exodus 14:14).

  B. Three forces wage war against the unbeliever:

    1. The world.

      a. The Bible warns us not to love the world (I John 2:15-17).

      b. No one who is in love with the world can be used of God in a significant way.

      c. We can have confidence of victory in this area for Christ has overcome the world. (John 16:33b).

    2. The flesh.

      a. The flesh—our old sin nature—is at war with the Spirit (Galatians 5:17).

      b. This conflict will continue as long as we live.

      c. Temptation (the initial impression to do something contrary to God's will) is not in itself sin. It becomes sin as we meditate on it and desire develops into lust, which is often followed by an actual act of disobedience.

      d. The conflict is resolved as we surrender continually to the control of the Spirit (Galatians 5:16).

    3. The devil.

      a. Satan is a real foe, seeking to destroy us (I Peter 5:7,8).

      b. We have the assurance that "greater

       is He who is in us than he who is in the world" (I John 4:4b).

   c. Satan was defeated 2,000 years ago at the cross and God's power is sovereign over him (Acts 4:28).

   d. God's spiritual armor provides our safety against Satan (Ephesians 6:11,12).

III. KNOW YOUR RIGHTS AS A CHILD OF GOD.

A. It is impossible to know and experience our resources in Christ without spending time with the Lord, who is the source of our strength (Ephesians 6:10).

B. Good works are a result of a life of faith (James 2:22).

C. Jesus Christ, in all of His resurrection power, actually lives within the Christian (Romans 8; Ephesians 1:19-23; Colossians 1:27-2:10).

D. We are weak in our own strength but strong in Christ (Philippians 4:13; II Timothy 1:7; I John 4:4, John 15:4,5).

E. As we learn of and draw upon our resources in Christ, we will be enabled to be the fruitful witnesses He commands us to be (John 15:8; Matthew 4:19).

   1. It is our responsibility to follow Him.

   2. It is His responsibility to make us effective fishers of men.

F. The resurrection power of Christ is available to every Christian to help carry out the Great Commission of our Lord (Ephesians 1:19-23; Matthew 28:18-20; Hebrews 13:5).

G. If we have Christ, we have everything we need, for we are complete in Him (Colossians 1:15,16,19, 2:3,8-10).

H. In Romans 5 and 6 we have an explanation of how God's resources become available to us when we receive Christ (Romans 5:19-21; 6:1-3,6,11,13,16).

I. Though God does not force us to obey Him contrary to our wills, the more we understand our resources in Christ, the more we will desire to do God's will. For in Christ we can do all things (Philippians 4:13).

IV. LIVE BY FAITH

A. We do not live by feelings; we live by faith (Hebrews 11:6; Galatians 3:11).

 1. Valid feelings are the by-product of faith and obedience (John 14:21).

 2. To seek an emotional experience repudiates God's command to live by faith.

B. As Christians, the object of our faith is made known through His Word.

 1. We can trust the great promise of God's Word that all things work together for good if we love God (Romans 8:28).

 2. On the basis of this promise, we can logically follow His command in I Thessalonians 5:18 to give thanks in all things.

C. God has commanded us to cast all of our cares upon Him (I Peter 5:7).

D. The best way to demonstrate faith is to give thanks in all things.

 1. This pleases God (Hebrews 11:6).

    2. Unbelief displeases God (Hebrews 3:17-
       4:2; Romans 14:23).

  E. From the time we awaken in the morning
     until we go to bed at night we should walk
     with God, trusting Him and thanking Him
     for every circumstance of our lives.

These Transferable Concepts are designed to make an important contribution toward your spiritual growth, but they are no substitute for the Word of God. If you do not already have a regular time when you study the Bible, we encourage you to begin one. To help you get started, a brief outline that you may want to use in your study follows. Simply select a short passage of Scripture and use the next four steps:

Observation. What do you see in this passage of Scripture? What does it tell you?

Interpretation. What does it mean?

Application. How can you use this in your life? What steps are needed to put this into practice?

Correlation. How does it fit in with other Scripture verses? (It is important to keep sections of Scripture in context with the entire scope of the chapter or book.)